Some Days Are
Lonely

Published by

MAGINATION PRESS

An Educational Publishing Foundation Book

American Psychological Association

750 First Street, NE

Washington, DC 20002

For more information about our books, including a complete catalog, please write to us, call 1-800-374-2721, or visit our website at www.apa.org/pubs/magination.

Printed by Phoenix Color Corporation, Hagerstown, MD

Library of Congress Cataloging-in-Publication Data

Kim, Young-Ah.

 Some days are lonely / written by Young-Ah Kim ; illustrated by Ji-Soo Shin.

    p. cm.

 "Originally published in Korean language as Some Days Are Lonely, copyright EenBook Co., 2011."

 ISBN 978-1-4338-1287-3 (hbk. : alk. paper) — ISBN 978-1-4338-1288-0 (pbk. : alk. paper) 1. Loneliness in children—Juvenile literature. 2. Loneliness—Juvenile literature. I. Shin, Ji-Soo. II. Title.

 BF723.L64K5613 2013

 158.2—dc23

                          2012035886

Manufactured in the United States of America

10 9 8 7 6 5 4 3 2 1

Some Days Are
Lonely

by Young-Ah Kim • illustrated by Ji-Soo Shin

Magination Press • Washington, DC
American Psychological Association

This English edition is published by arrangement with EenBook Co., through the ChoiceMaker Korea Co.

No matter how hard I look,
it feels like there is no one around.

I call out loudly,
but no one answers.

Sometimes it feels
like there is only me.

I am lonely.

Slop, plop. Slop, plop.

My steps feel heavy,
sinking deep into the mud.

Like cotton dipped in water,
my heart feels damp.

My heart sometimes fills
with dark clouds, just like the sky.

I hear rolling thunder:

Rumble, rumble, rumble.

I know, some days...
some days are lonely.

Lonely days when it feels like I am the only one under the heavy, heavy skies that are about to rumble.

Days when it feels like the sun has disappeared.

I want to weep.
I want to wail like a baby.

Sniff, sniff.
Sob, sob.

But then I remember that dark clouds can lift from the skies and can lift from my heart, too.

A clear sky can appear and the sun can once again shine.

There might even be a rainbow!

Splash!

Lonely days can arrive unexpectedly.

We all have those days.

But don't forget: As the clouds pass,

you might find a rainbow!

Little Bear's expressions match the weather. Can you match Little Bear's expression with the right weather picture?

If your heart were like the weather, what kind of weather would it be today?

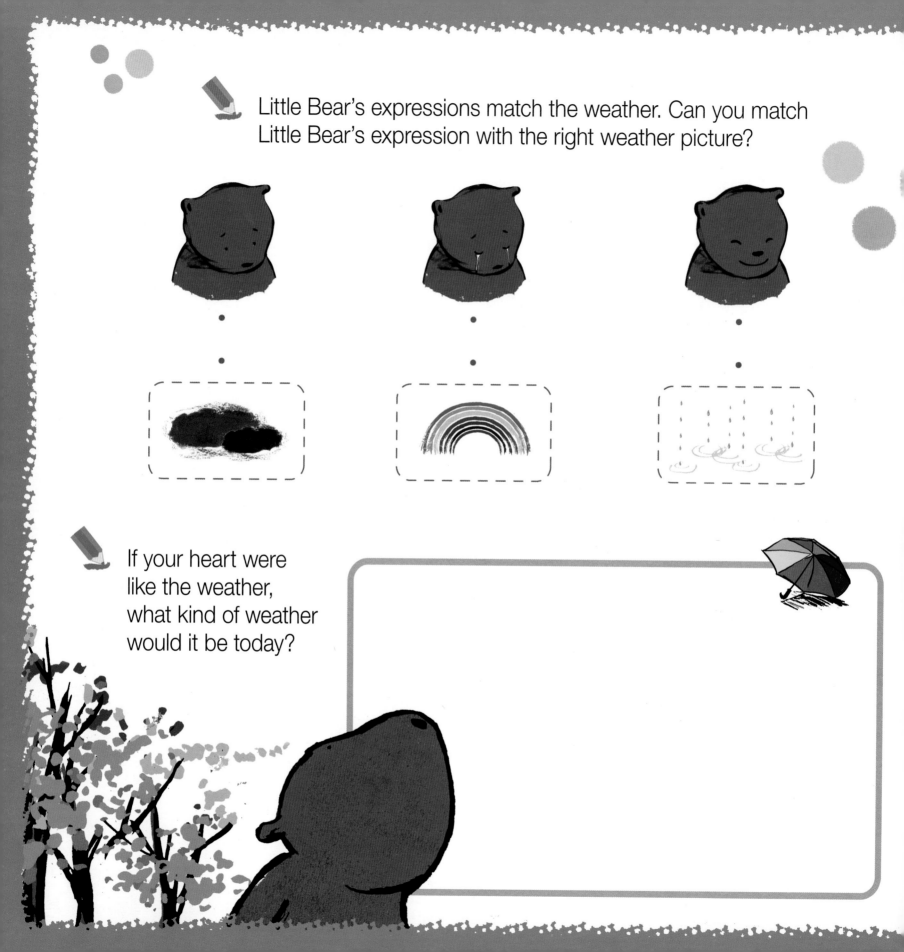

When you are lonely, what would make you feel happier and better? Draw your answer.

 The window is open. If a friend would come by, happy to see you, which friend would you like to see? Draw that friend's face in the window.

Note to Parents

A child may experience the emotion of loneliness when she has a need or desire to be interpersonally connected and recognizes that connection is missing. Loneliness may be triggered by the lack of a satisfying relationship, or by alienation, isolation, or exclusion from one's peers. In any case, loneliness can result in feelings of emptiness, inferiority, vulnerability, helplessness, and a sense of longing for someone to really know you. If a child is without friends she may wish to have someone in her life who will relieve the emptiness. Yet loneliness can exist even when a child has numerous friends, as those connections may be fleeting, meaningless, or unfulfilling. Thus, a child may have many friends, or be in a room filled with other children, and still be lonely.

How Loneliness Feels

Loneliness, like all emotions, creates certain thoughts. It can cause a child to imagine that everyone else has the kinds of affiliations that he strongly desires, or that other children are enjoying the company of friends while he is feeling inadequately connected. His longing for closeness may, at times, lead him to believe that his situation might never end. It's understandable why children who are lonely might feel unwanted, unloved, undesirable, insignificant, despairing, insecure, or abandoned—they are trying to make sense of their lonely feelings, and these attributions account for their lack of connection, however falsely. How a child perceives himself when he is lonely can either motivate him to initiate a relationship or cause him to be more hesitant to reach out to others. Such hesitation on the part of a lonely child can result in further isolation, as well as the possibility of rejection or victimization by peers.

Emotions are immediately and briefly experienced, and they differ from the prolonged states that define moods. A lonely mood is akin to a lingering sadness, but with a particular referent; it's sadness about not having someone in your life with whom caring and deep understanding is mutually felt. Even so, a prolonged state of loneliness can lead a child to feel bored, estranged, or depressed. Some children who experience a lonely mood will appear to be sad. However, others may respond aggressively to a lonely mood, and, rather than appear to be sad or bored, will instead be agitated, hostile, or defiant.

Aloneness and Loneliness

It is important to distinguish aloneness, or solitude, from loneliness. Either one can be experienced without the other. Solitude can be a pleasant experience that allows a child to think, be creative, rest, or simply pass time in an activity. Solitude may trigger anxiety for some children, but this is different than the experience of loneliness, as are situations in which a child prefers to be alone in order to avoid anxiety that might be experienced in social activities.

Strategies to Help Defeat Loneliness

If your child appears sad, bored, emotionally withdrawn from her peers, or if she is agitated and upset, engage her in conversation. She will likely be more prone to reveal personal information to you as you tuck her into bed, or if she is otherwise engaged with you in a mutual activity, such as walking the dog or driving to the grocery store. You may say something like, "It seems like you've been quieter lately. I notice you haven't joined in with the other kids at the playground. Is anything going on? I'd like to help." Inquire about friendships and if she is satisfied by them or if she is lonely when it comes to her relationships. If she reveals information that leads you to believe she is lonely, you can offer some of the following suggestions:

Take risks socially. Suggest that your child socially take some risks— for example, make eye contact, sit at a lunch table with others, engage in conversation with children who are around him in class, or request a play date with a peer. Since asserting himself socially is something he must do in order to overcome loneliness, the best role of a parent or caregiver is an encouraging one where the child feels safe to discuss the outcome of his attempts to socialize. Let him know that you will be there for him to discuss the results of his risk-taking.

Self-disclose. Engaging in conversations with others is essential in order to defeat loneliness. Although part of social interaction has to do with being skilled at drawing out the other person, it is just as important to self-disclose in order to form a connection with a peer. Help your child find interesting "talking points" about herself that she can convey to others in her conversations with them. For example, you may say something like, "Talking about yourself is hard, but it helps others get to know you and be interested in who you are. Maybe at recess tomorrow you can talk to Susie about what you thought about the reading assignment, or your dog, or something funny that happened to you."

Be responsive. Loneliness can lead to self-absorption and a high sensitivity to possible rejecting behaviors of others, causing a child to hopelessly avoid others or desperately seek their positive affirmation, all the while ignoring the needs of the other person. For this reason, in social interactions, it is important for your child to remain mindful of the needs of others when he is lonely. Using examples in your own life or those present in the child's life, such as a relationship with a sibling or her other parent, help your child recognize the needs of others and be responsive to them. For example, you may say, "Your brother loves talking to you, and I know he wants to hear about your day at school. But I think he'd also like to talk about his soccer game. Maybe you can ask him how it went."

Avoid avoidance. Help your child recognize that loneliness is an emotion that, like all emotions, provides you with information about your environment and current concerns. Loneliness is trying to tell you something: namely, that you are missing important connection with others. Avoiding social situations, or not doing something about your present circumstances, is not listening to what your emotion is advising you to do. You may tell your child, "It's always hard to take a risk and talk to others, but it's the only way to feel less lonely. It may take a while, but if you keep reaching out to others you can find a good friend. I'll always be here if you want to talk to me about how it goes."

It is normal for a child to feel lonely occasionally. With time, and with your help, your child should be able to overcome her loneliness and return to her happy self. However, if the feeling persists, becomes overwhelming, or interferes with daily activities, it may be time to seek help from a licensed psychologist or psychotherapist.

Mary Lamia, PhD, *is a clinical psychologist and psychoanalyst in Marin County, California. She is also a professor at the Wright Institute in Berkeley, California.*

About the Author

Young-Ah Kim is a children's physical education instructor and children's story writer. Her stories include *Where Is My Jar of Honey?*; *When Spring Comes*; *Slowly, Step by Step*; and *The Giant Outside the Window*. She firmly believes books strengthen the heart and looks forward to sharing more heart-warming and beautiful stories with her readers.

About the Illustrator

Ji-Soo Shin studied painting and illustration in school. Shin's picture books include *Porcupine Story* and *Grandma Can't Even Lay an Egg*. Shin used crayons for *Some Days Are Lonely*, then colored with Photoshop.

About Magination Press

Magination Press is an imprint of the American Psychological Association, the largest scientific and professional organization representing psychologists in the United States and the largest association of psychologists worldwide.